PEARABLES

by R. HAYES SEAMAN and R. HAYES

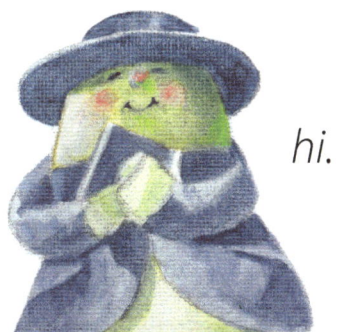

hi.

This is not a book about drawing pictures of pears, but it is about picturing pears and drawing them.

Robert Hayes Seaman, father of Robin, is a painter, drawer and teacher of drawing (pears and other things).

Robin Hayes, daughter of Robert, is a packaging, marketing and publications designer.

Both currently live in Keene, NH.

See more of their work at 368Art.com

Images ©2017 Robert H. Seaman

For our family and friends,
wherever they may be.

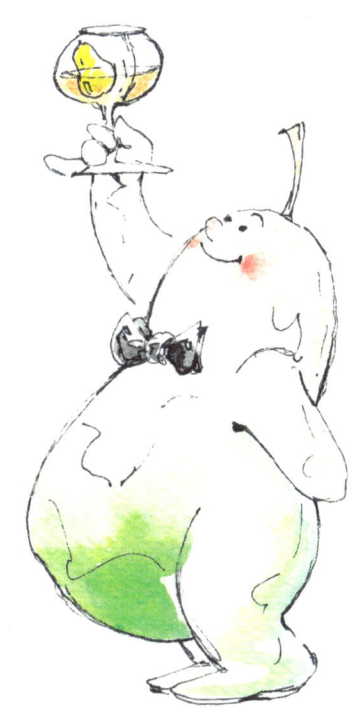

Pear's to you!

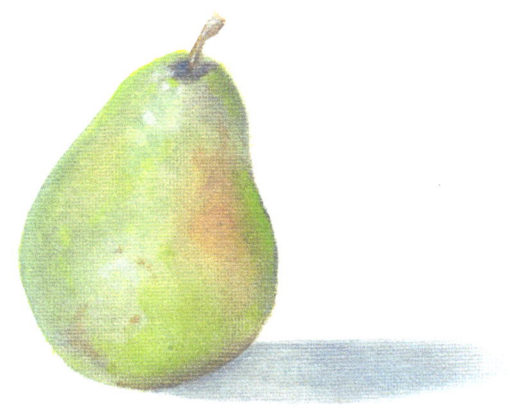

Q: Is that a pear?

A: *No it isn't.*

Q: Really? It looks like a pear.

A: *Well it isn't. It's a picture of a pear.*

Q: Oh, I see. Is it a copy of a real pear?

A: No, I just copied the pear in my head.

Q: WHAT!? There's a pear in your head?

A: Not exactly. I made a picture of a pear in my head and copied that. I can think up all kinds of pear pictures and draw them.

Q: You can?

A: Sure. I'll bet you can too. Just close your eyes for a sec and "think" pear. What do you see?

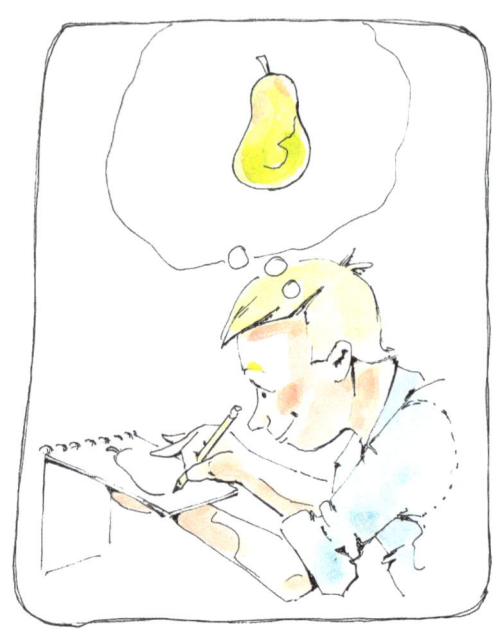

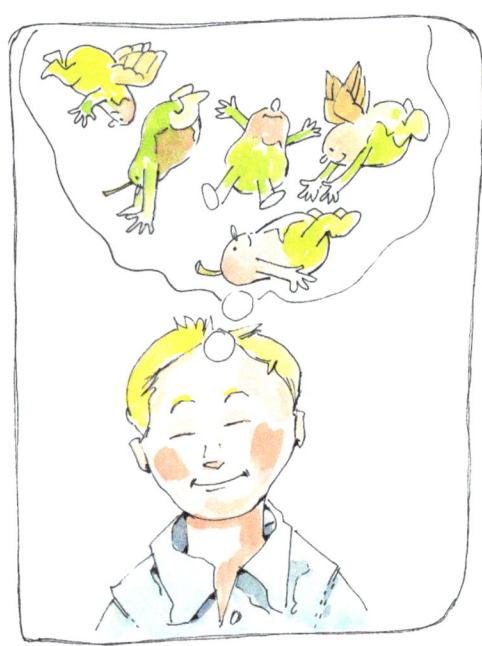

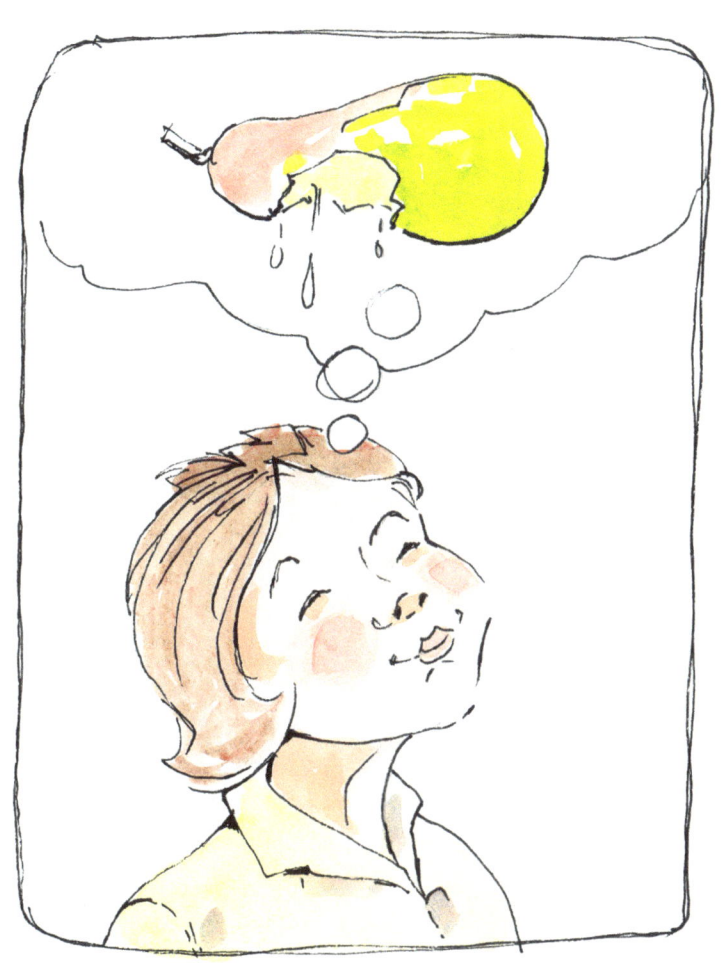

Q: Wow! I see a juicy pear and I just took a big bite out of it. Yum!

A: *So let's dream up some pear pictures and draw what we see.*

Q: Okay. You first, big fella.

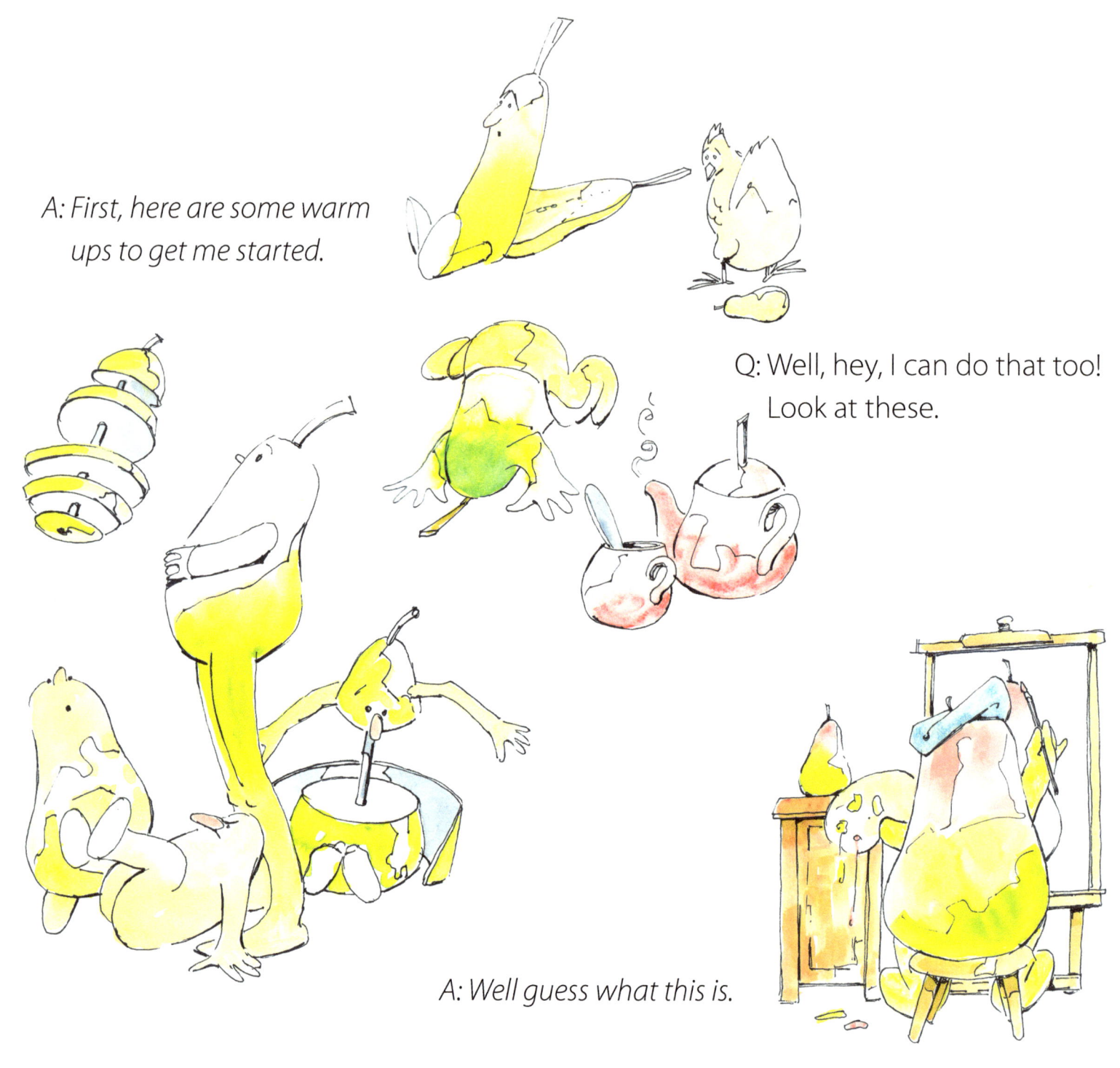

Q: That's easy. That's a picture of a pear painting a picture of a pear.

A: *Bravo! How about this one. Guess what it is.*

Q: I don't know. Tell me.

A: *Just this one and you'll have to guess the rest.*

Q: Oh, okay. What is it?

A: *It's a pear juice factory!*

Q: Well I'll be! My turn.

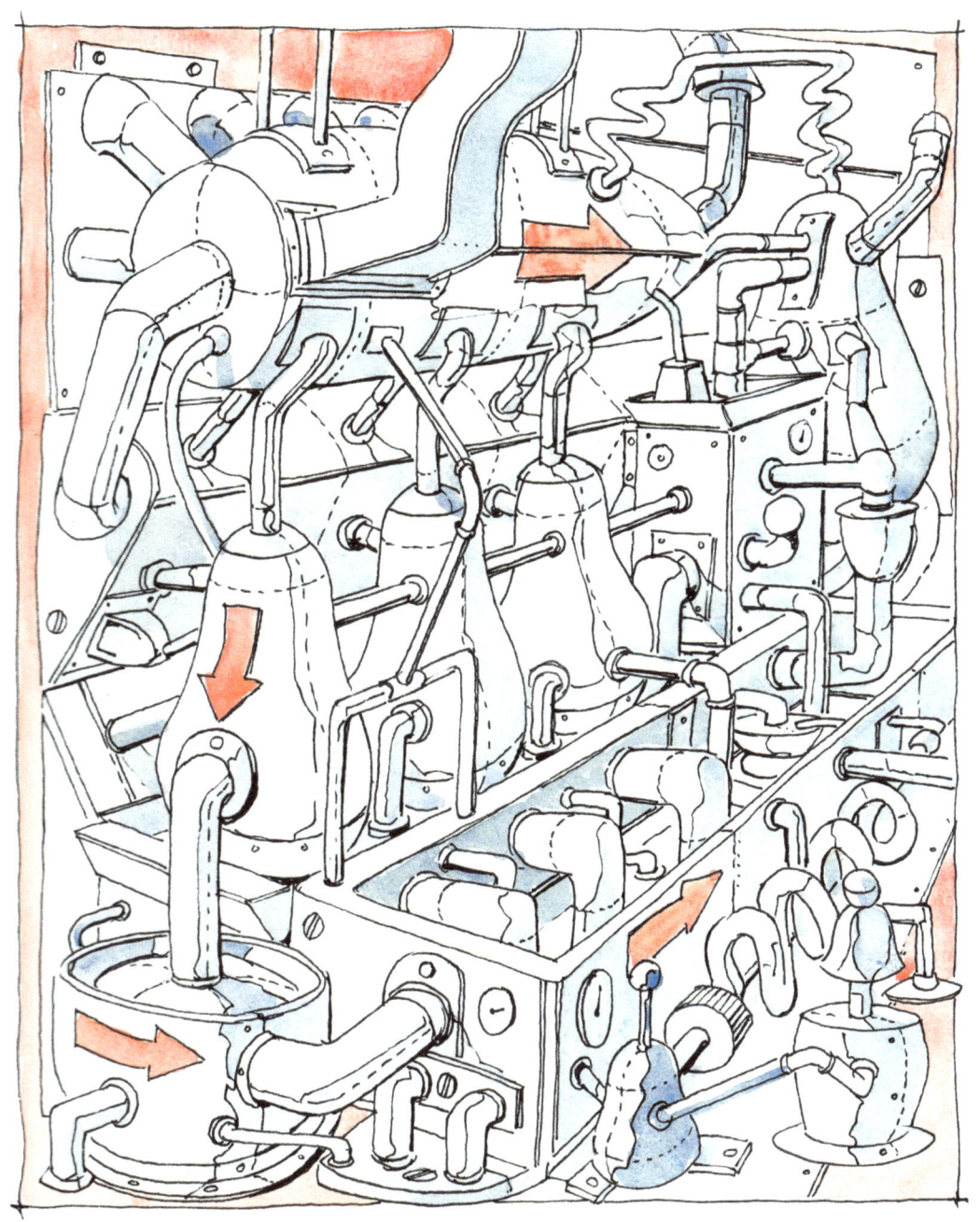

Q: So, look at this one. Don't know what to tell you. It just popped up and grew on it's own. Don't know what to make of it...or call it.

A: *Hmmmm...don't know what to call it either. Sometimes you just sit back and open the door to your imagination. Sometimes it's amazing what walks out.*

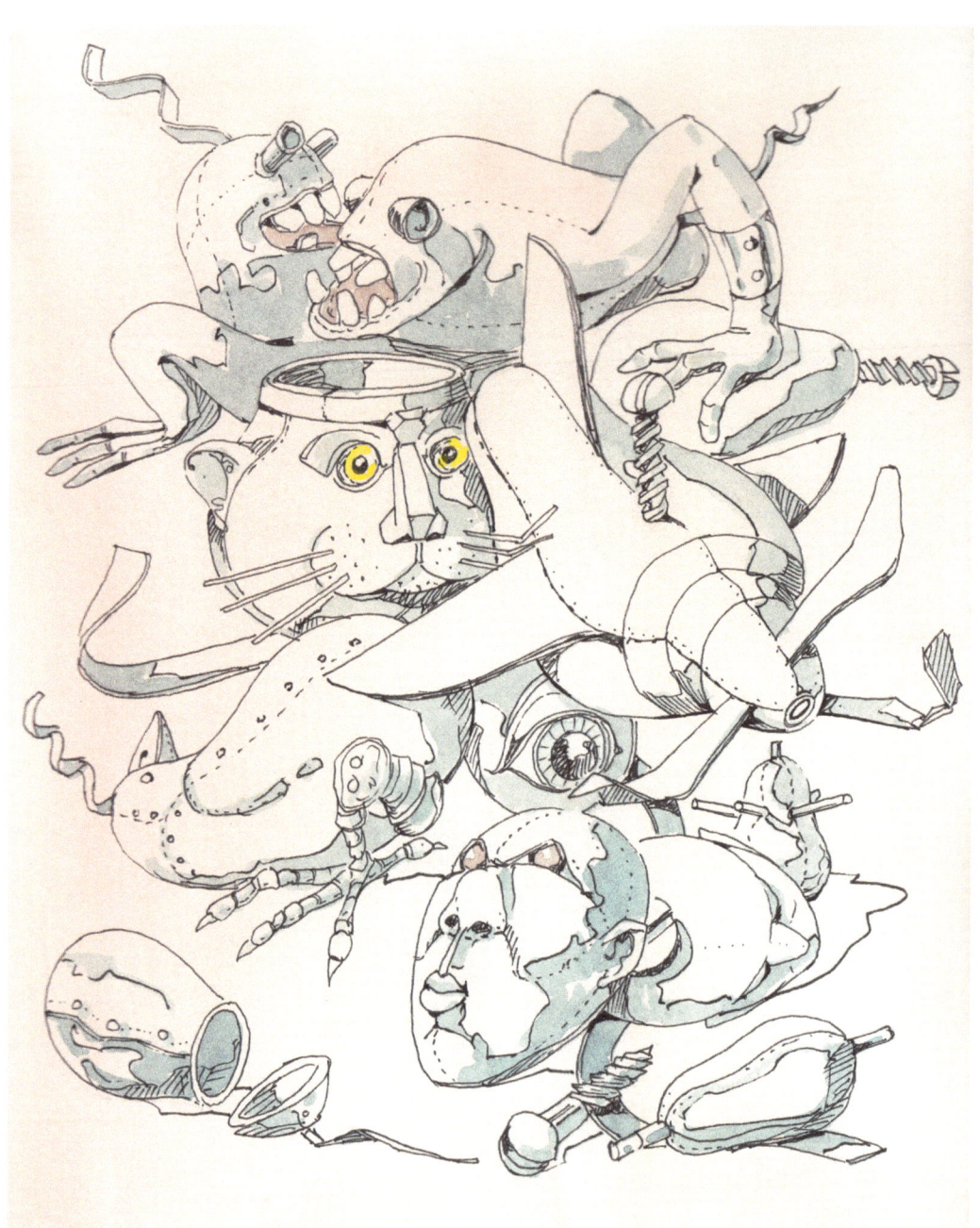

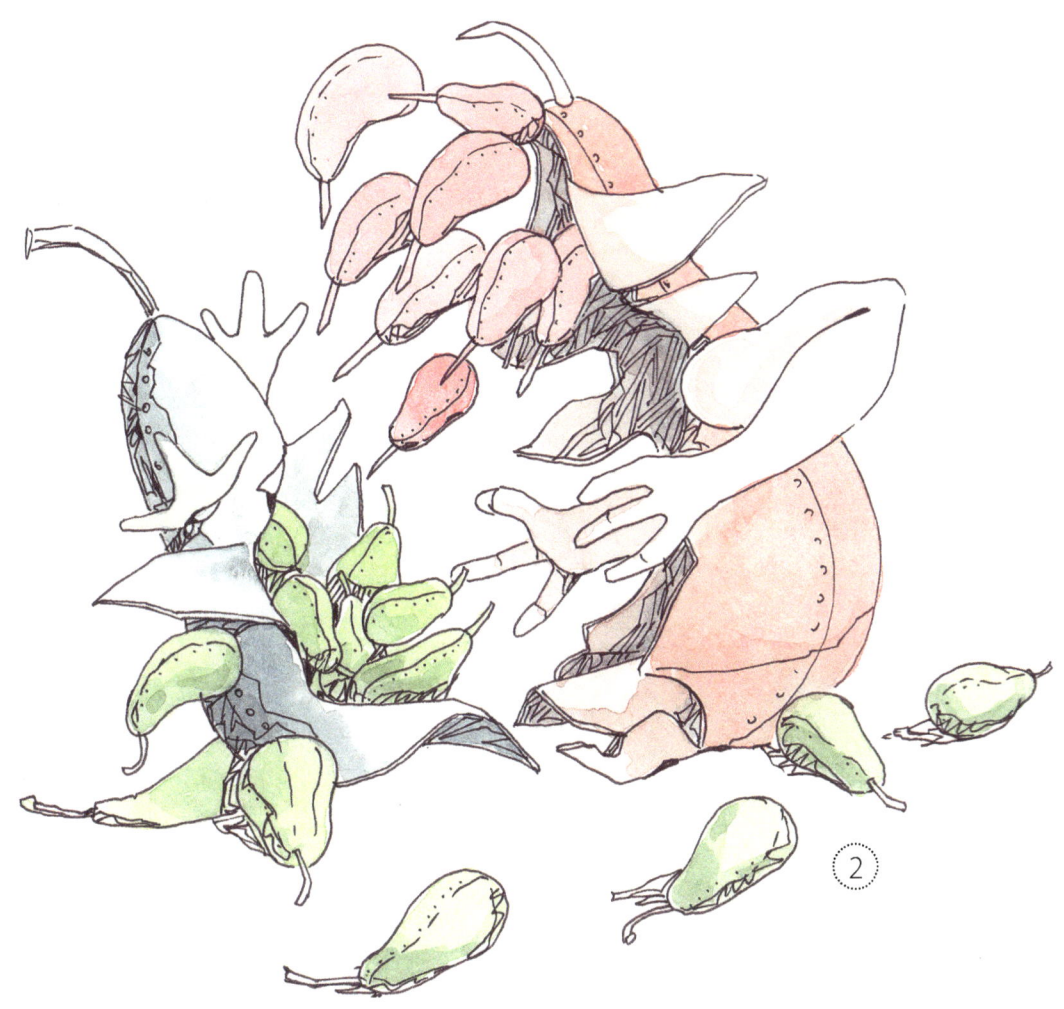

A: Like this! What is going on here?

Q: Yikes! It looks like the big guy is really screaming at the little guy. I can almost hear the little fellow crying, "I'm sorry! I'm sorry!"

A: Open the door a little wider and see what you get. Something a little lighter, like so...

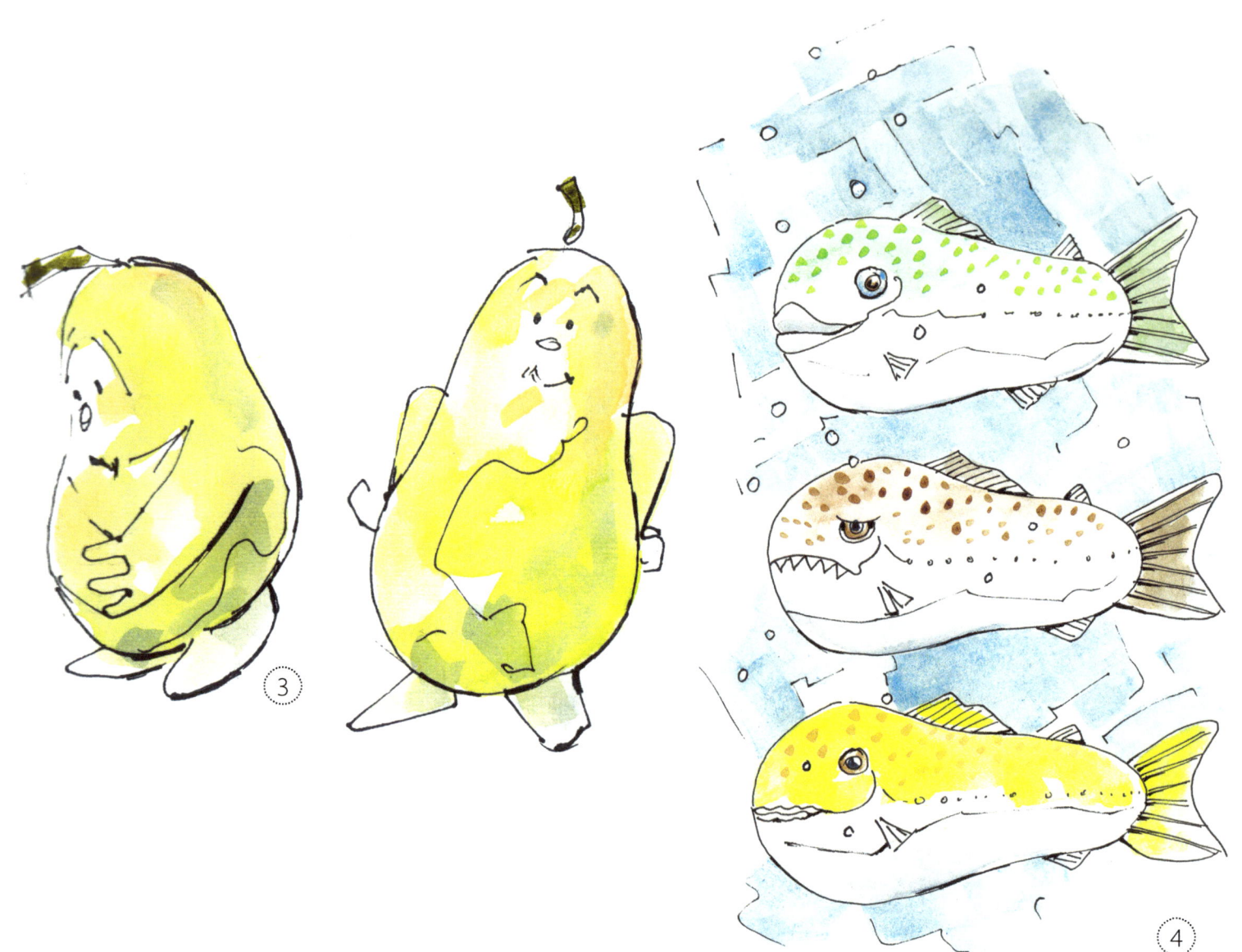

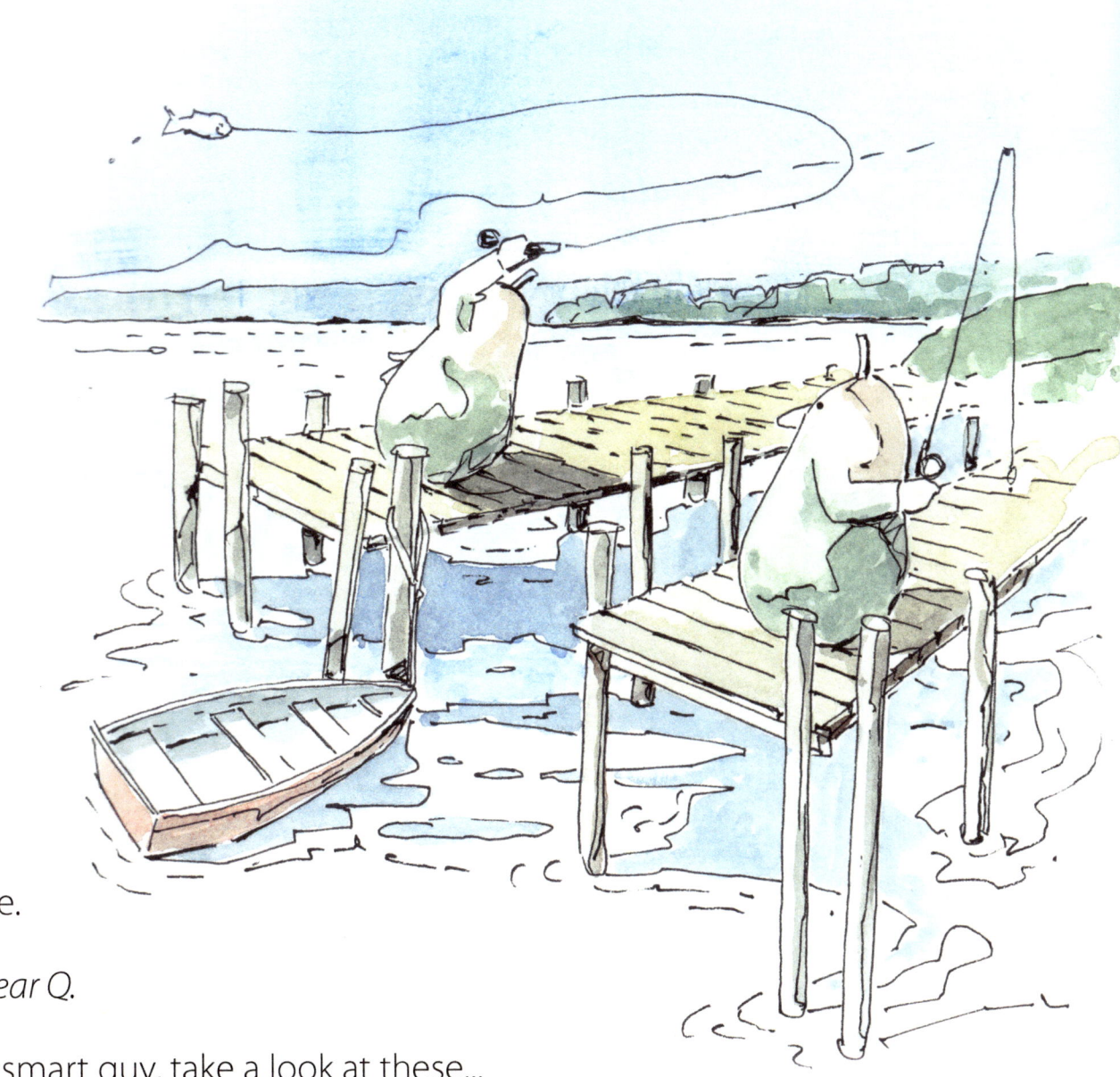

Q: Tell me...please.

A: *No. Later on, dear Q.*

Q: Really!? Okay, smart guy, take a look at these...

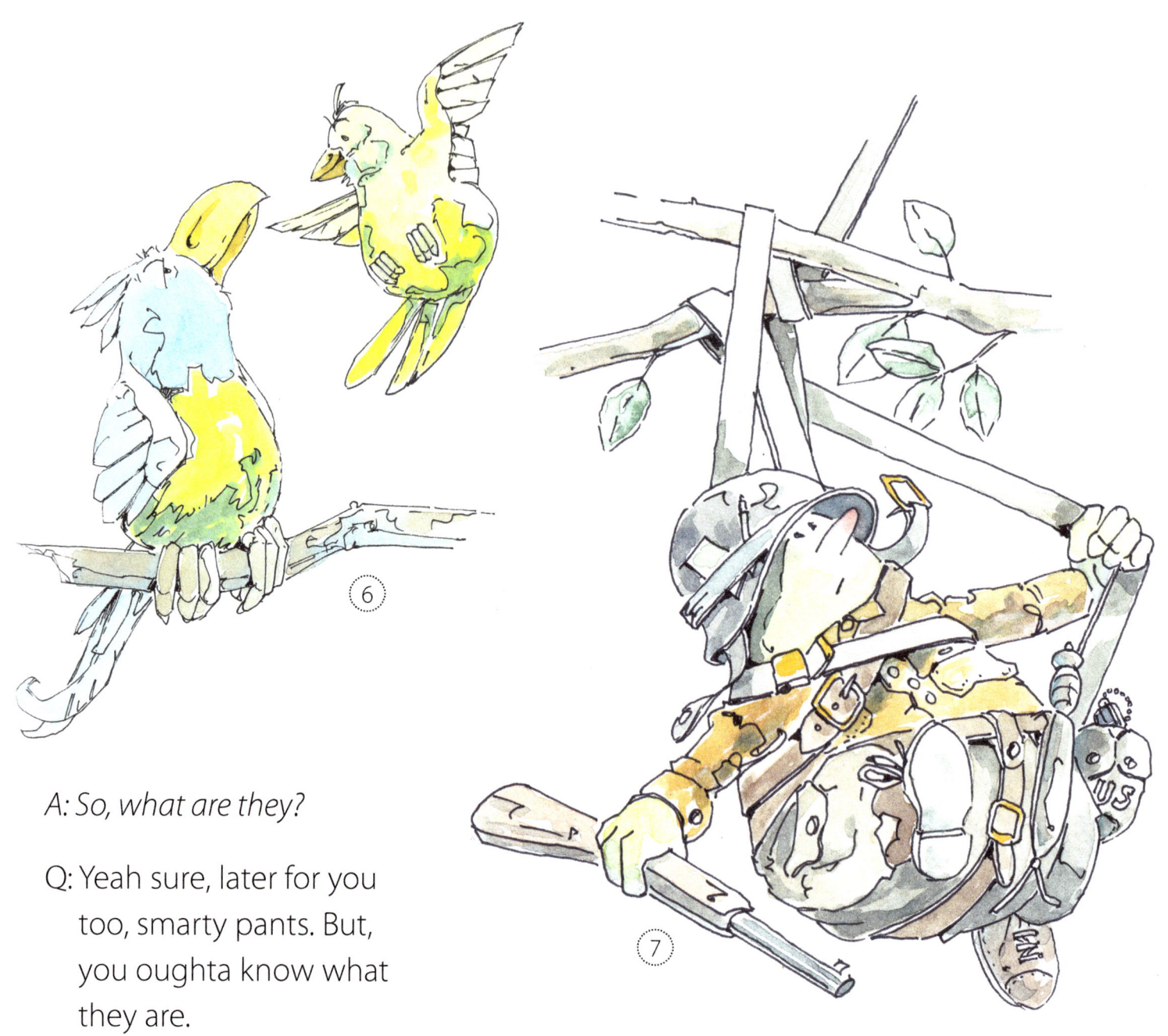

A: *So, what are they?*

Q: Yeah sure, later for you too, smarty pants. But, you oughta know what they are.

A: Hah! I know a pearatrooper when I see one. But the birds... hmmmmm. Well, try these on for size.

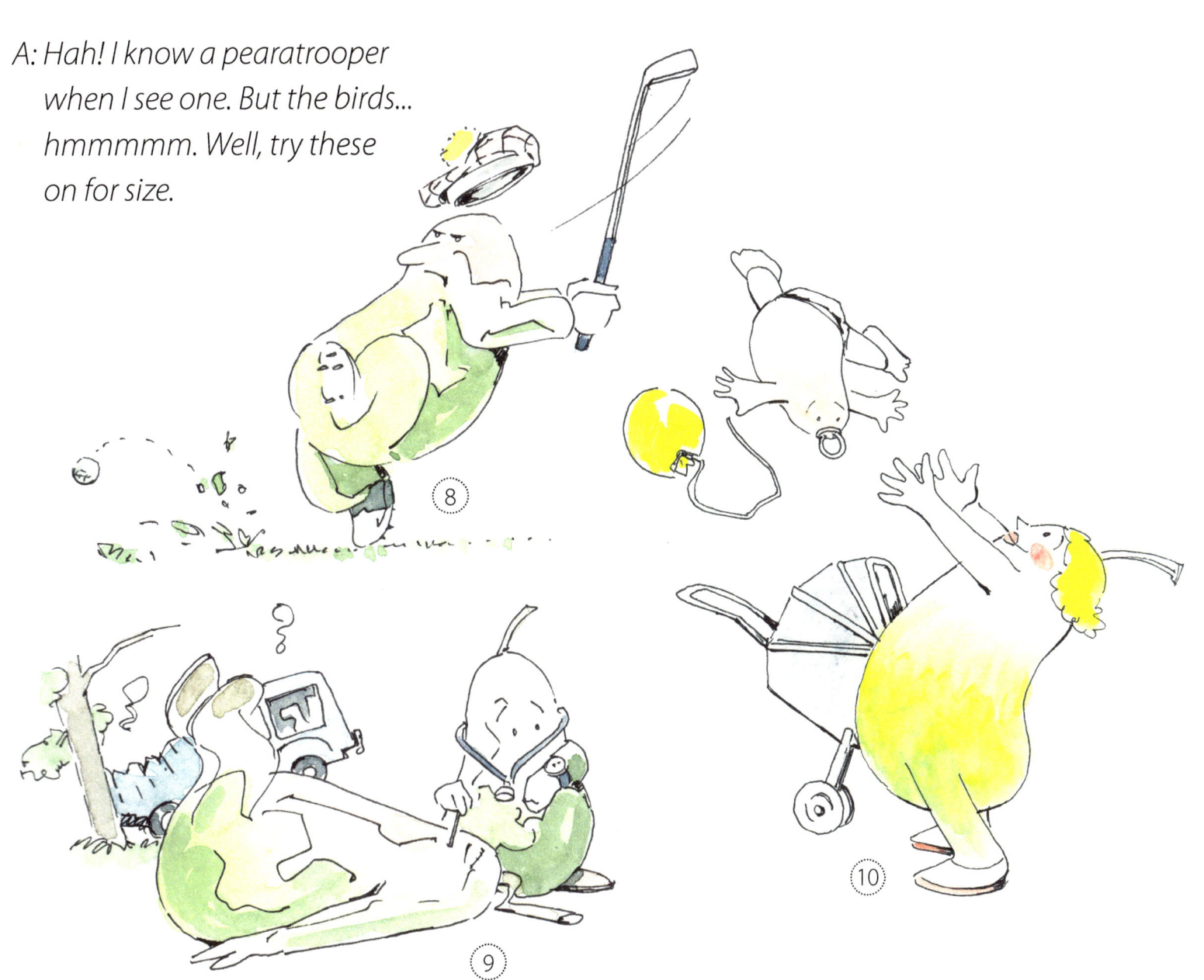

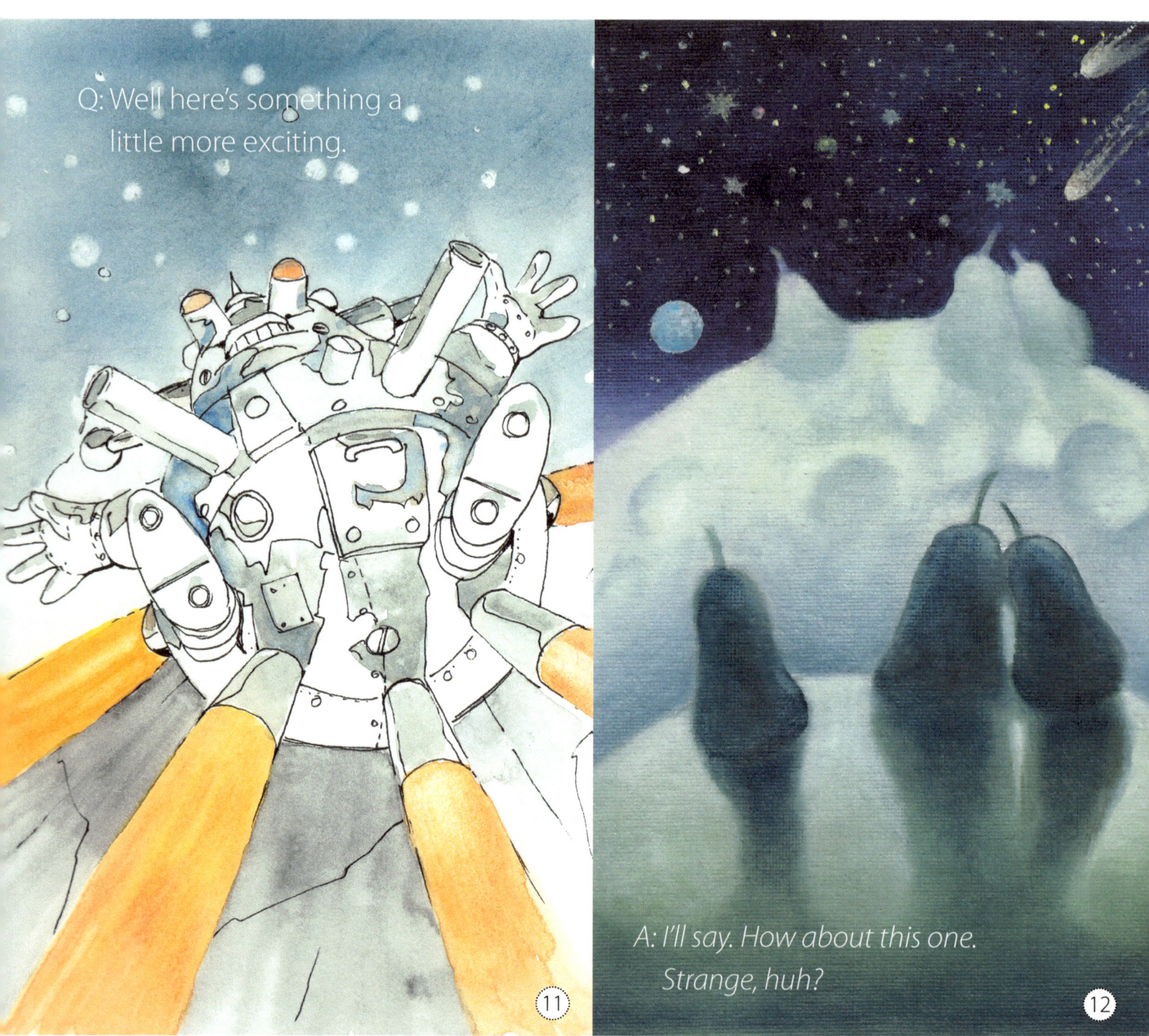

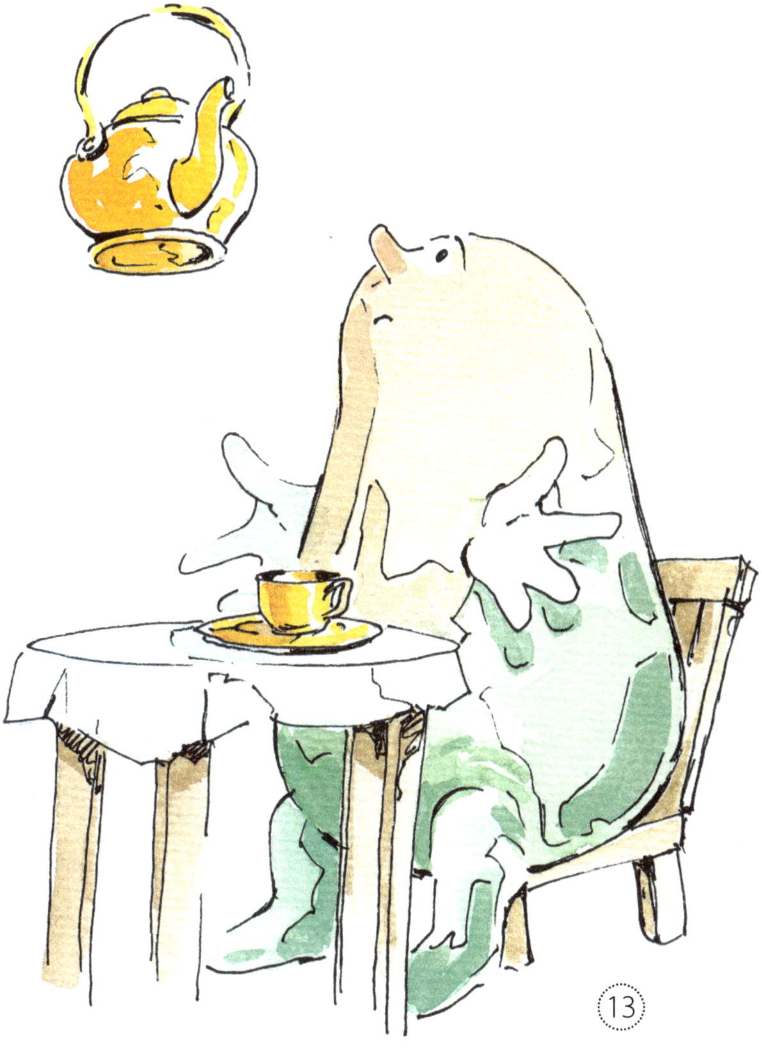

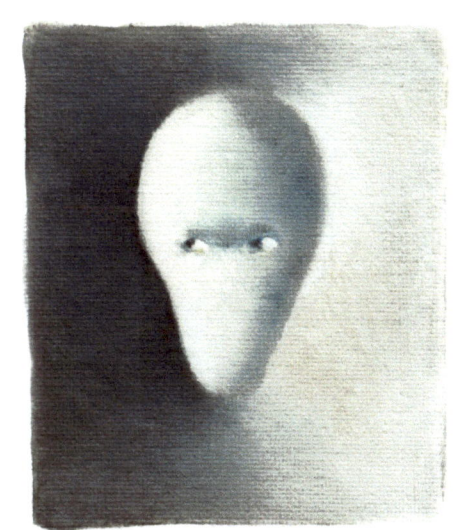

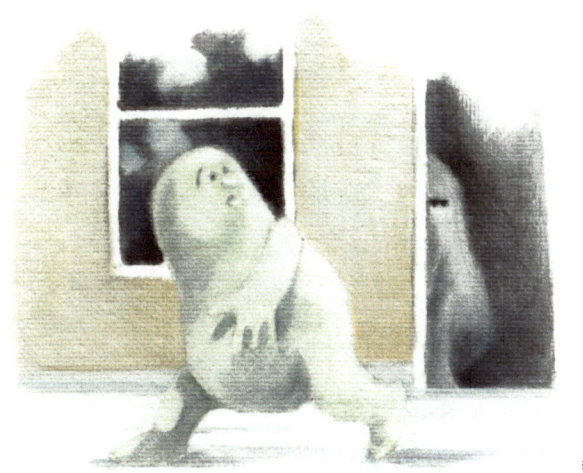

Q: ooooh...creepy too. Let's lighten things up a bit with these...

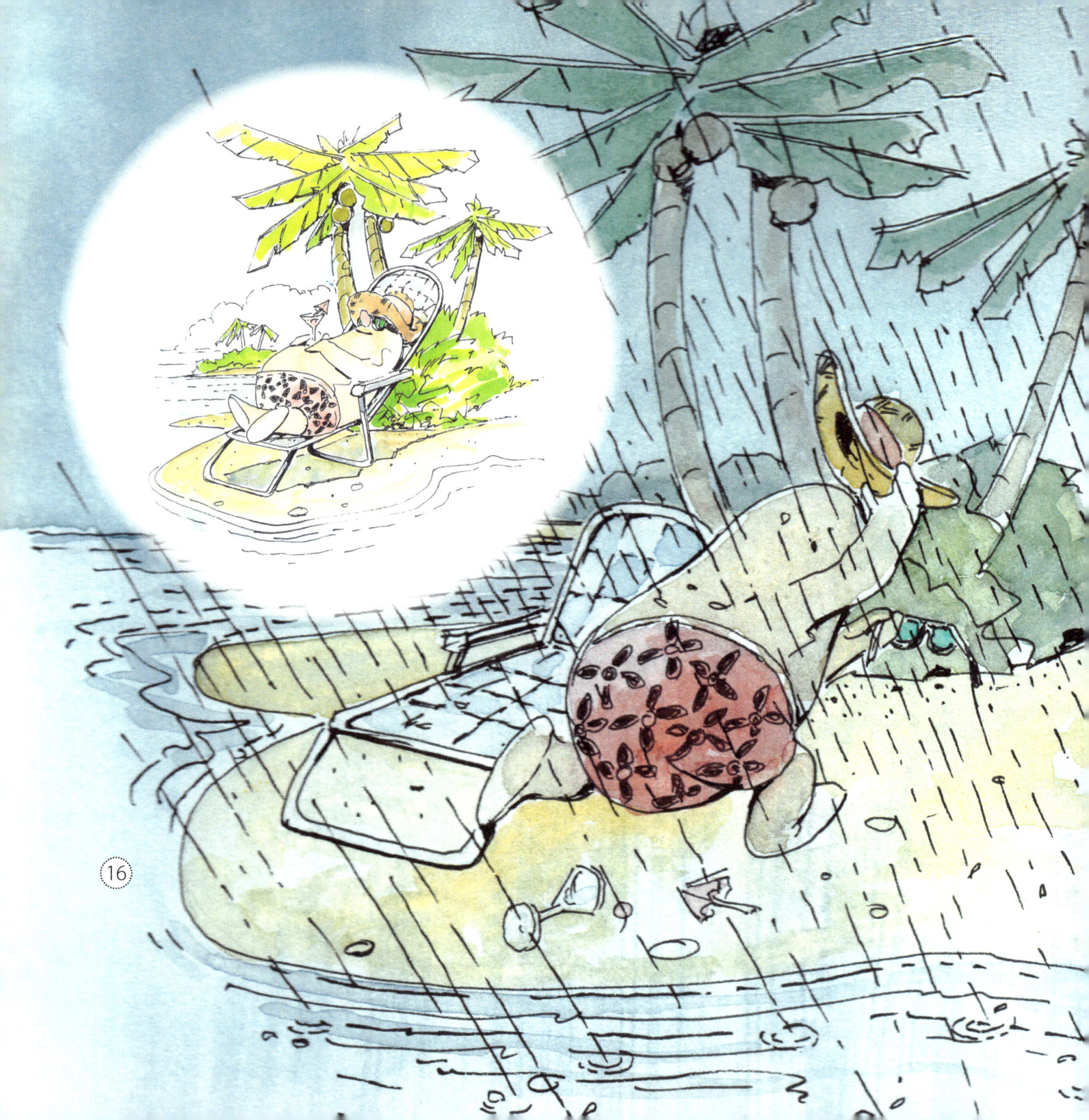

Q: You know, this is great fun but I'm beginning to think enough is enough.

A: Oh, okay, but just a few more. Pears of all kinds keep coming through the door. You'll never get this pear... I mean pair.

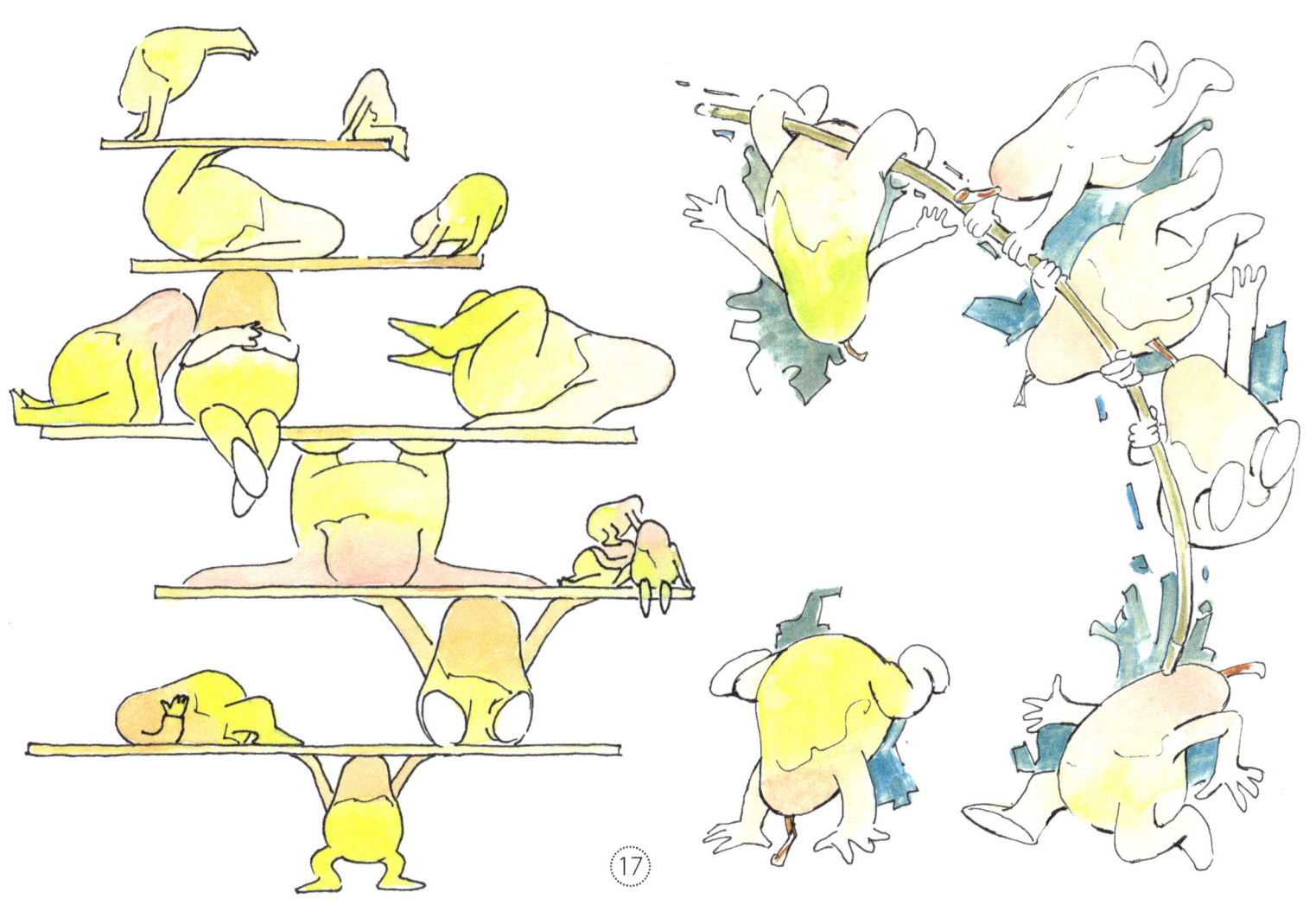

Q: Well, if you must, here are some last gasps from me too... go figure.

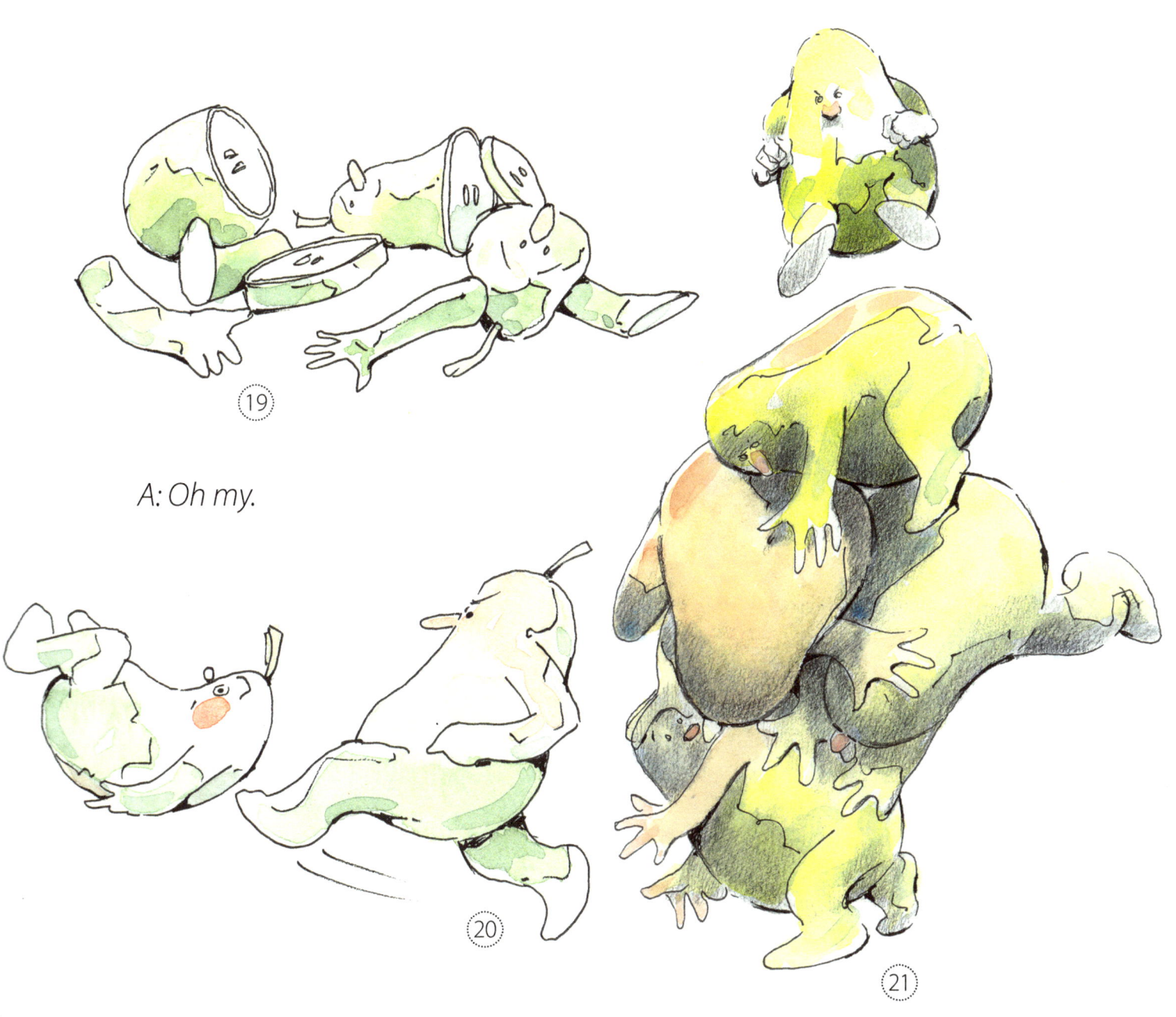

A: *Oh my.*

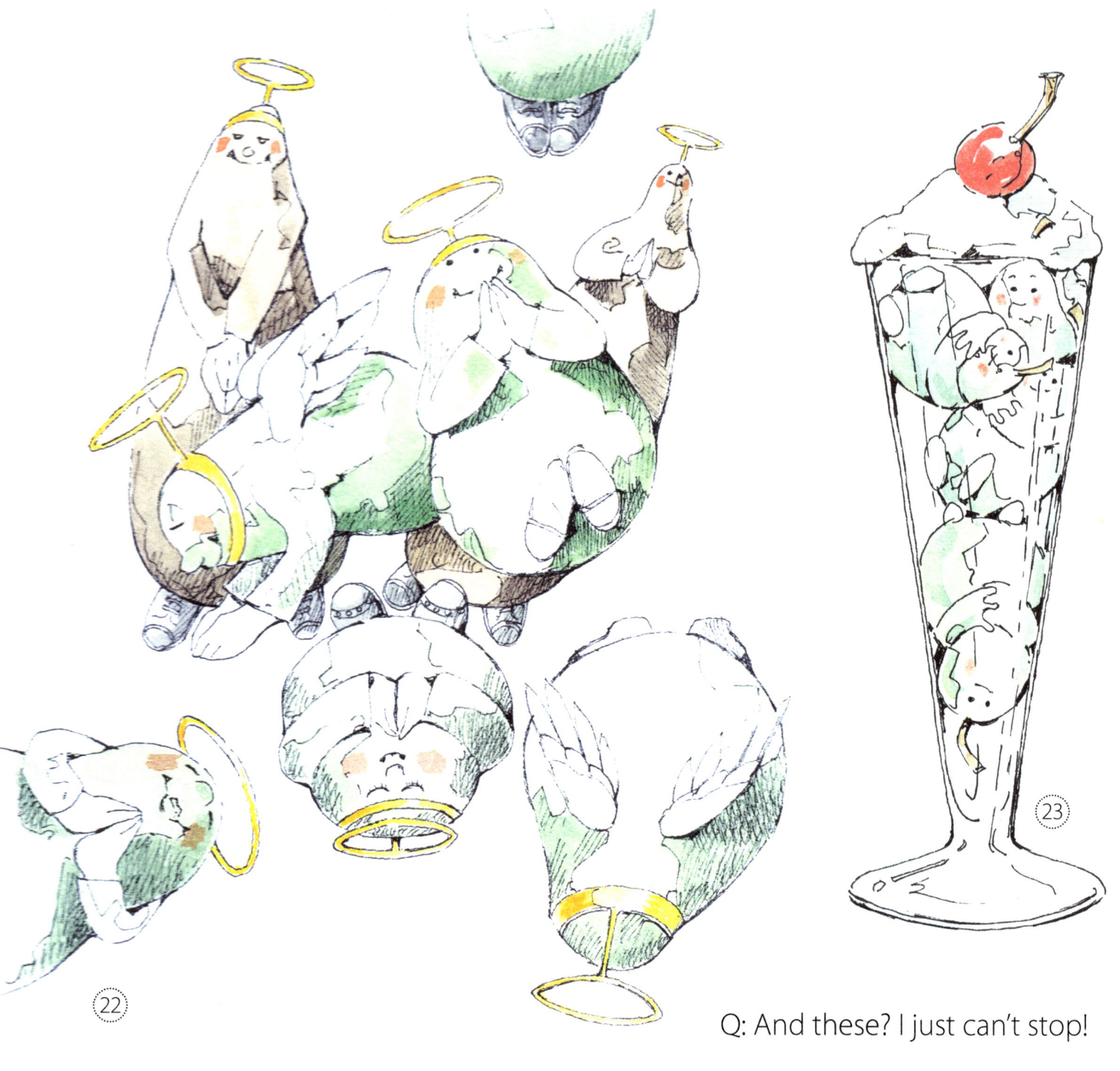

Q: And these? I just can't stop!

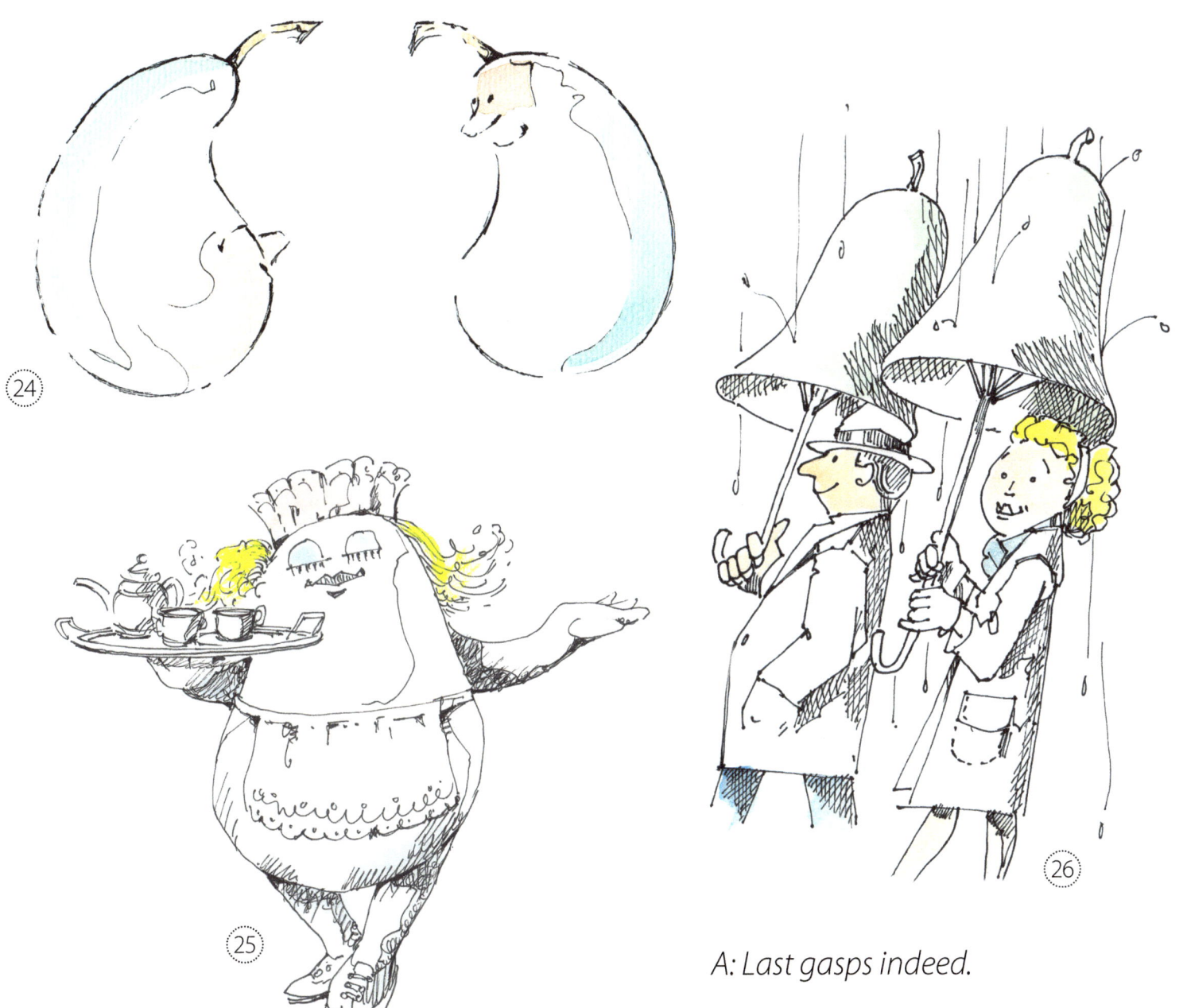

A: Last gasps indeed.

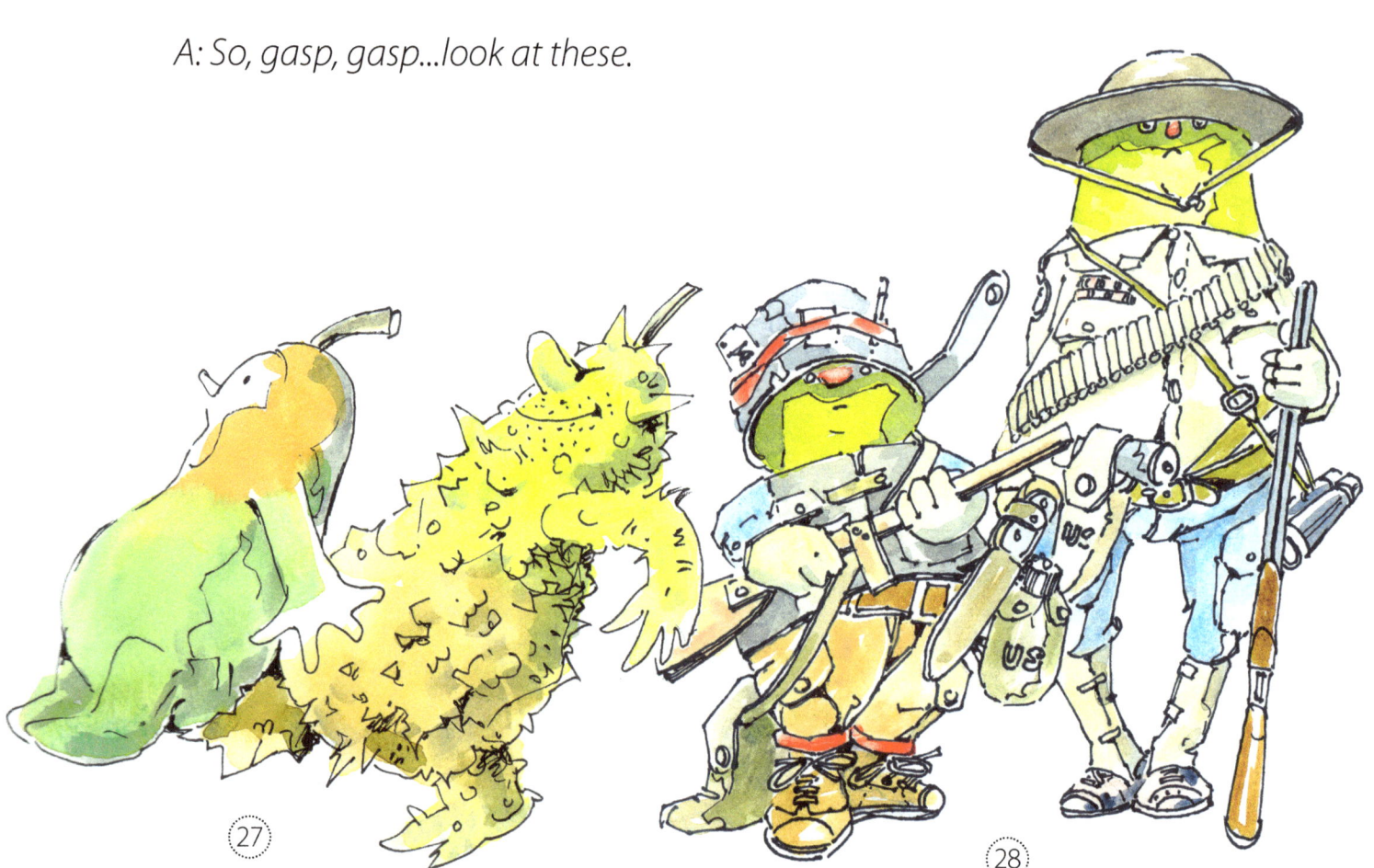

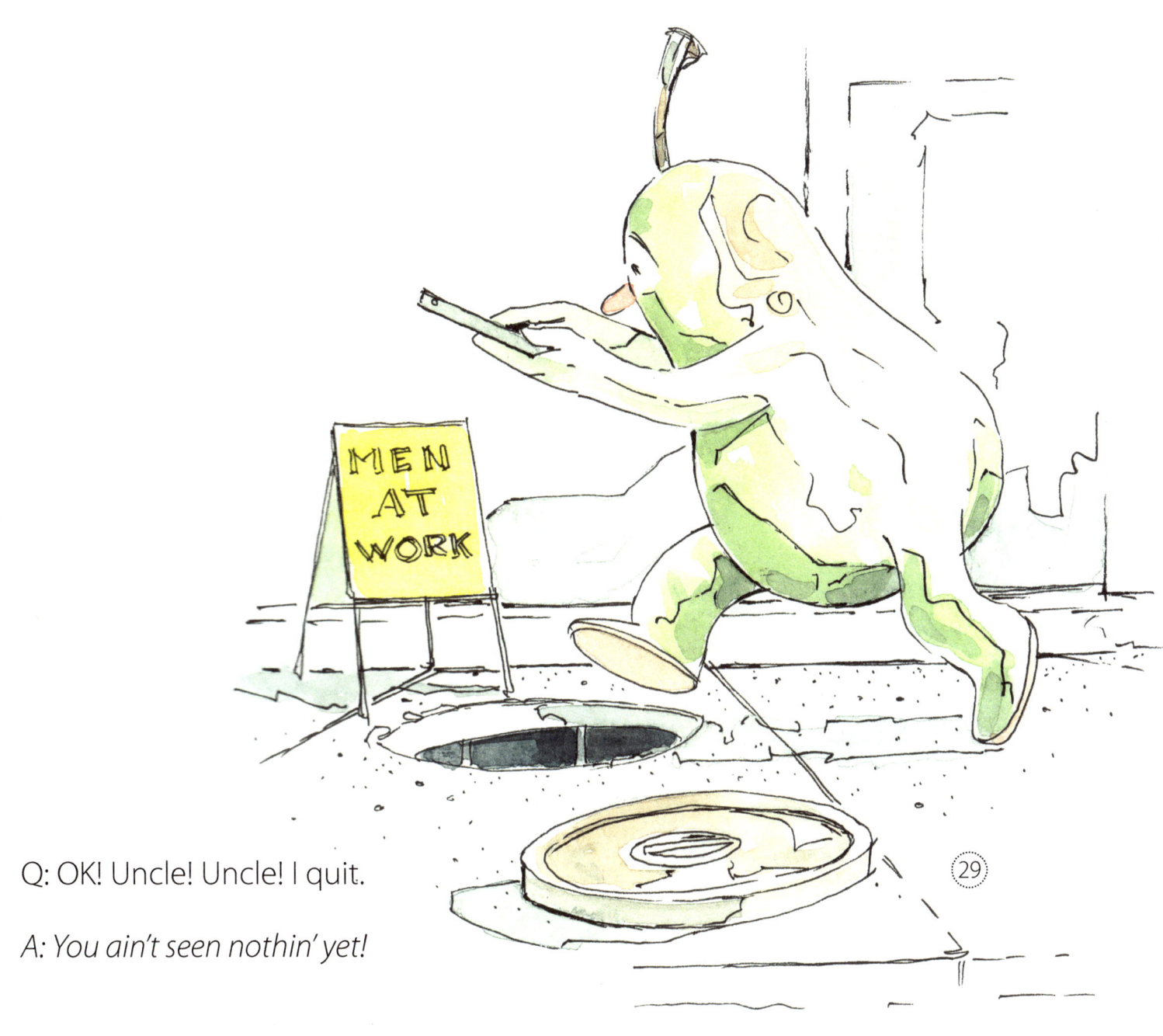

Q: OK! Uncle! Uncle! I quit.

A: You ain't seen nothin' yet!

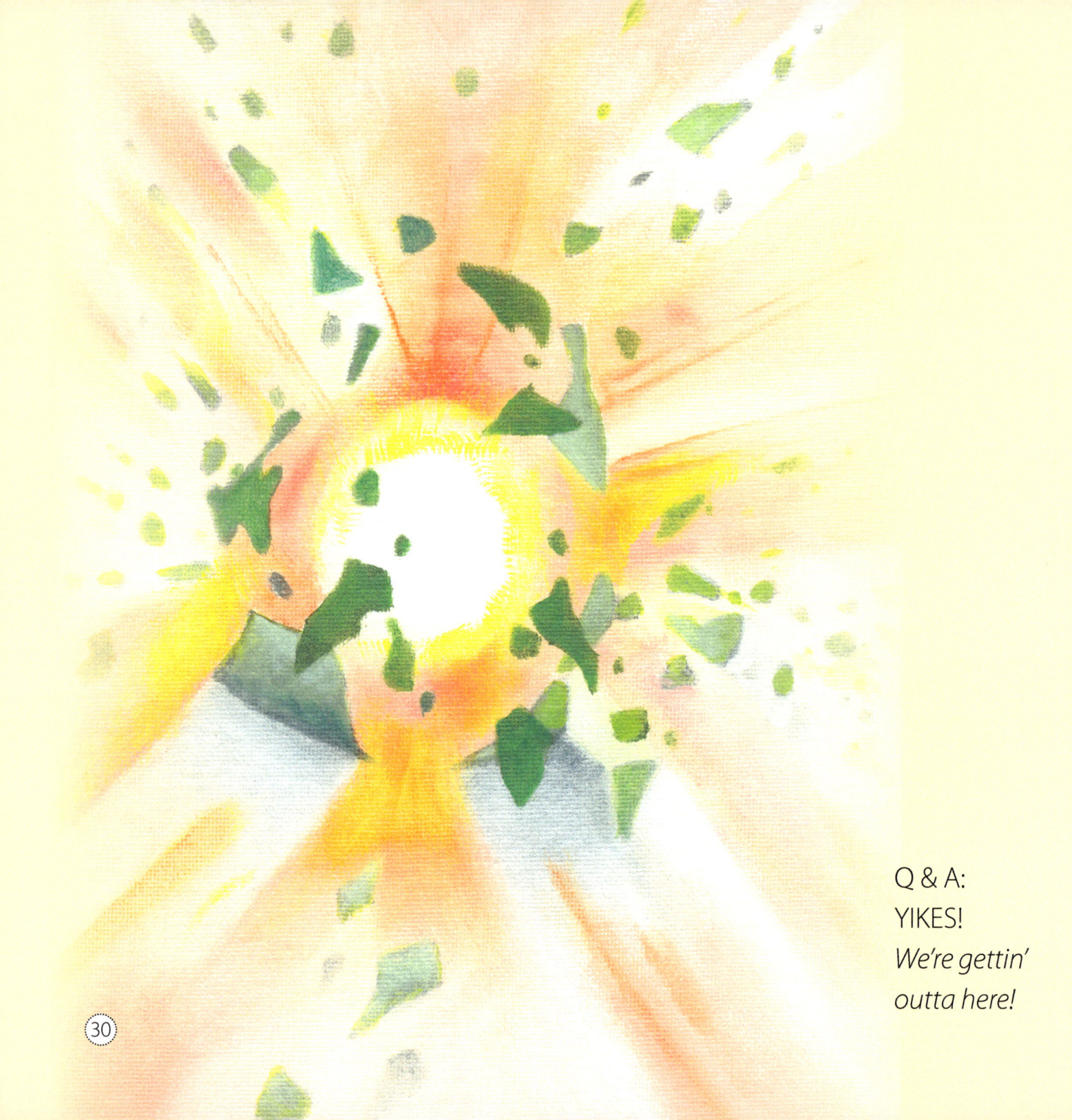

Q & A: YIKES! *We're gettin' outta here!*

finito (almost)

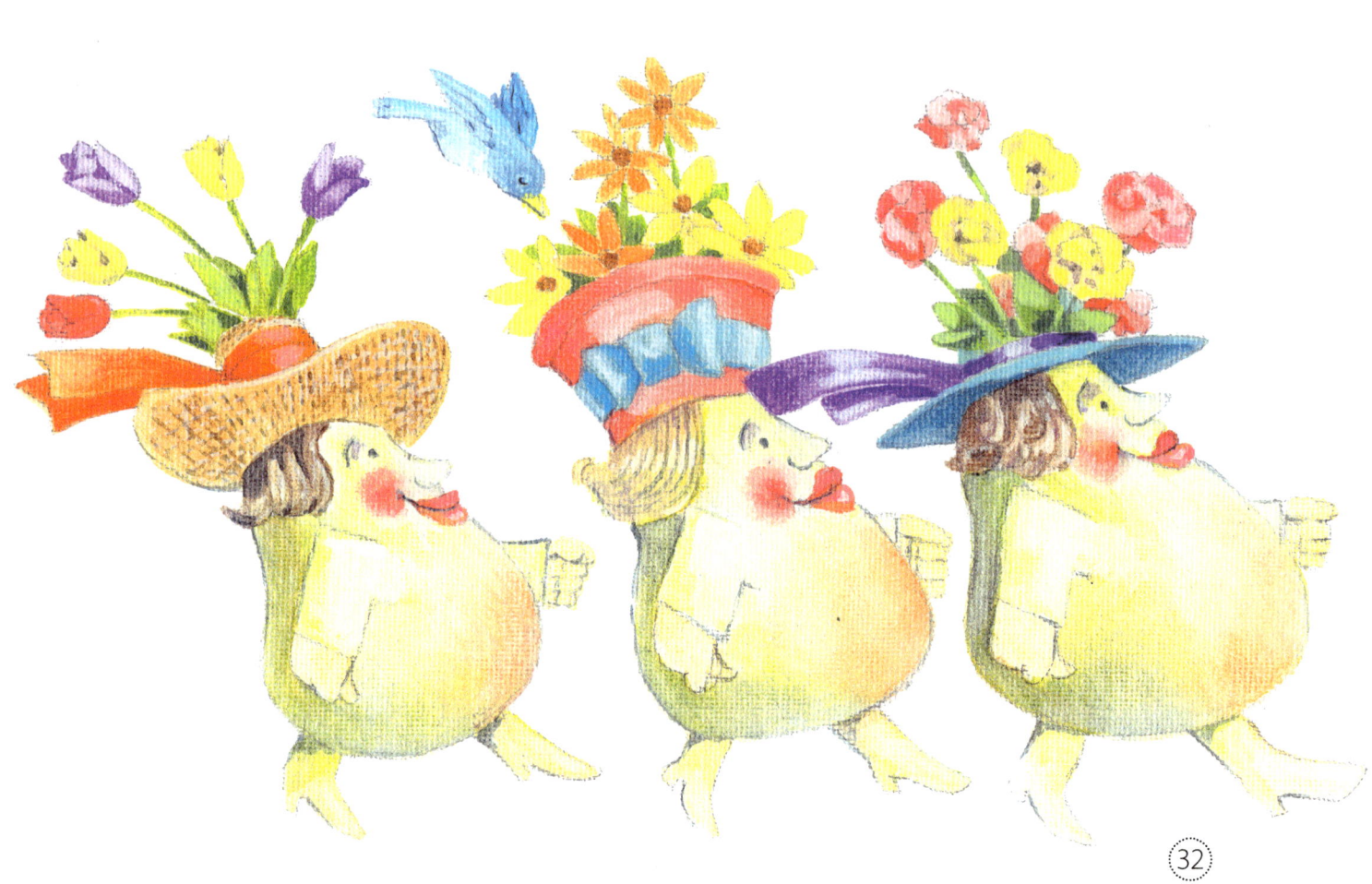

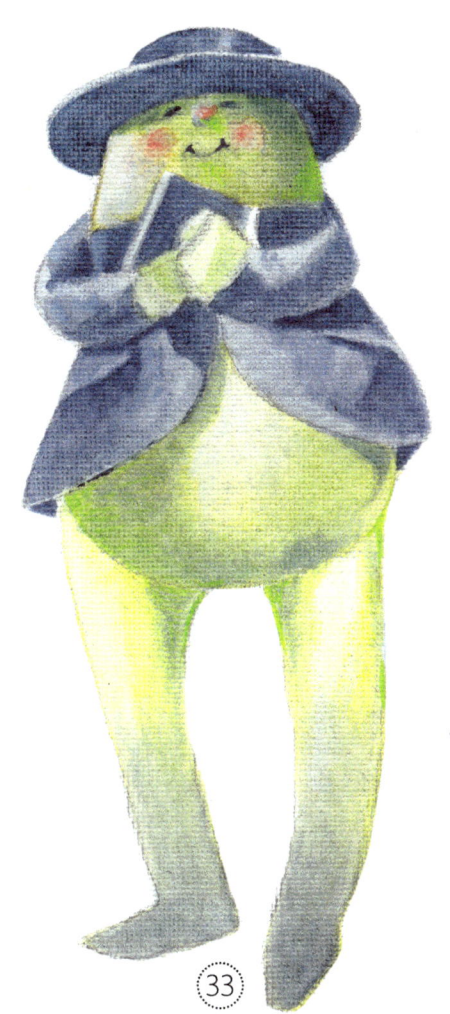

...and this is how you do it.
But turn the page...
...and bless you.

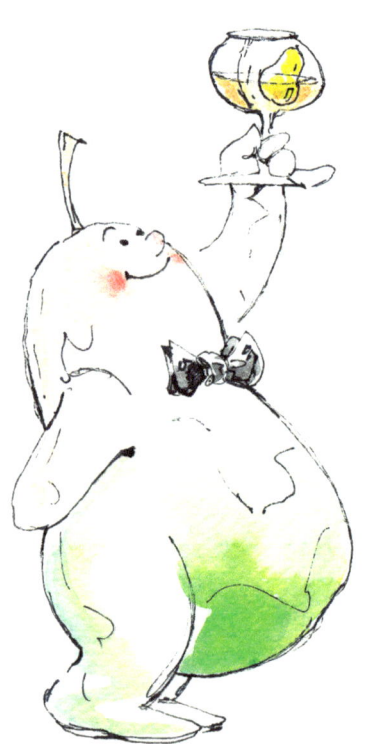

So, here's what they are...in case you need help.

1. No clue
2. Ditto
3. Despear and Datpear
4. Pearrot Fish, Pearanha, Pearch
5. Pearadox
6. Pearrot & Pearakeet
7. Pearatrooper
8. Pear for the Course
9. Pearamedic
10. Au Pear
11. Couldn't tell you.
12. Pearallel Universe
13. Pearanormal
14. Pearanoia
15. Sense of Pearil
16. Pearadise & Pearadise Lost
17. Cirque du Pear
18. Pearambulator
19. Pear Parts
20. Pearental Guidance
21. Pear Pressure
22. Pearagons of Virtue
23. Pearfait
24. Pearenthesis
25. Pearlor Maid
26. Pearasols
27. Prickly Pear
28. Pearamilitary
29. Pearilous Situation
30 & 31. Here are a couple pears that won't be making it back to the library.
32. Easter Pearade
33. Pearish Priest

www.ingramcontent.com/pod-product-compliance
Lightning Source LLC
Chambersburg PA
CBHW051825210526
45473CB00005B/1743